I0058469

The McNeill Factor

WORKBOOK

How to Start and Run a Successful MasterMind Group

ANN MCNEILL

©2018 Ann McNeill
All rights reserved

ISBN 978-0-9837566-5-1

No part of this book may be reproduced, stored
in a retrieval system, or transmitted in any form
or by any means, electronic, mechanical,
photocopying, recording or otherwise without
the written permission of the author.

Published by

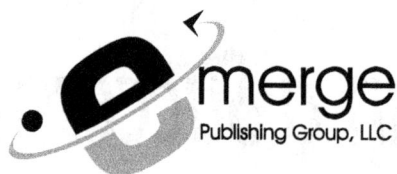

Emerge Publishing Group, LLC
Riviera Beach, FL
www.emergepublishers.com
561.601.0349

Ann McNeill 2018
The McNeill Factor

Printed in the United States of America

This workbook belongs to:

Name:

_____

Address:

_____

_____

Email:

_____

Phone Number:

_____

From: _____ To: _____

Contract With Self

Your Commitment to Your Commitment

I, _____ hereby enter this agreement this _____

day of _____, in this year _____, and I agree to do the following:

- Complete my personal affirmation.

- Repeat my affirmation at least twice daily.

- Set goals for the current year, and write action items for completing these goals.

- Adhere to the accountability guidelines established by TMF.

- Allow TMF members to hold me accountable to the goals I set for myself.

- Commit to the achievement of my goals I have set for the year.

My Signature: _____

Today's Date:_____

Table of Contents

Introduction

We are so happy that you have decided to embark on this journey of creating balance in your life by using the The McNeill Factor (TMF) Ten-Step System. TMF is an ideal organization for anyone looking to grow personally and professionally.

To effectively MasterMind and fully leverage TMF's holistic approach to personal advancement, the members of TMF must be of a certain character and should have demonstrated a level of commitment to the other members, to their group and to the organization, as a whole. Each candidate must demonstrate: (i) knowledge of the organization and its principles; (ii) positive characteristics; (iii) a level of commitment to the organization and its tenets; and (iv) dedication to learning and self-improvement.

Now therefore go and I will be with thou mouth and teach thee what thou shalt say.
Exodus 4:12

NOTES:

_____

_____

_____

_____

_____

_____

_____

_____

_____

_____

_____

_____

_____

_____

_____

_____

_____

_____

_____

_____

_____

_____

_____

_____

_____

_____

_____

The MasterMind Concept

The premise of MasterMinding is based on Napoleon Hill's book, *Think and Grow Rich,* in which he explains the mastermind principle.

Each person is required to set his/her goals for six months, one year, five years and ten years. Weekly, you should be working towards the goals that are stated in your annual report.

The object of MasterMind is to show accountability. You must have goals and plans if you are going to succeed in any endeavor. Successful people have plans while failures never plan. Success consists of three ingredients:

1. **Direction:** Set your sights on things that are worthwhile in life. Establish a plan, and work toward the fulfillment and accomplishment of your goals.

2. **Balance:** Keep the proper perspective about every area of your life. Staying in harmony with the Creator produces perfect balance. Balance in all things produces joy.

3. **Belief:** No one will become successful if they do not possess belief. The greater your belief, the greater your degree of success. Great people are believers!

No one can stop a person with a plan because no one has a plan to stop him or her. Included in this workbook is a format for establishing yearly goals and a format for writing down your weekly goals. Be sure to write your affirmation before starting your yearly goals. In writing your affirmation, remember to visualize the person that you intend to become. Visualization adds value to everything. If you cannot see the person that you are going to be, then it is futile to write the goals until you can.

We have included testimonials of other MasterMind members in this workbook to help you get an idea of the impact MasterMind has in the lives of those who are serious about having a better quality of life. Our hope is that these testimonials will inspire you on your goal setting journey.

Remember those who fail to plan, plan to fail.

Where there is no vision, the people perish
Proverbs 29:18a

NOTES:

_____
_____
_____
_____
_____
_____
_____
_____
_____
_____
_____
_____
_____
_____
_____
_____
_____
_____
_____
_____
_____
_____
_____
_____
_____
_____
_____
_____
_____

TMF History

On the eve of a new year, a new era in life was ushered in for Ann McNeill. On December 31, 1980 instead of enjoying the New Year's Eve festivities out and about, McNeill decided to stay home and read a book. That book was Napoleon Hill's *Think and Grow Rich* and it changed her life. The book soon became her "bible" of sorts and like any religious zealot she took her bible with her everywhere she went. She "preached" its principles to anyone that would listen. She gave the book to a small circle of friends at her local church in West Palm Beach, and from there began to give the book as a gift for birthdays.

In *Think and Grow Rich* McNeill was introduced to the MasterMind concept of goal setting. Once she started to apply the principles in the book to her own life, a shift began to take place. She began to move from mediocrity to excellence. She also realized that it would be selfish of her to keep the MasterMind concept to herself, and a big part of MasterMind is accountability. She needed to share MasterMind with others. She needed a group of like-minded people to whom she would be accountable. She began to meet in discussion "sessions" with those to whom she had given the book. From this the original *MasterMind Women's Group* was formed.

As McNeill's life transitioned so did the group. Her move to Miami meant the formation of a MasterMind group in Miami in the early 1990s. The original Miami MasterMind women included Alice Fincher, Bert Johnson, Isabella Rivers, Shuandra Scott, Nifretta Thomas and, of course, Ann McNeill. The group quickly expanded to include five more ladies (Gail Seay, Juanita Dawsey, Lawanda Scott, Tanya Jackson, and Mia Merritt.) who all cemented and held together over the next decade. For ten years, this group met every Saturday morning at 7:00 to discuss their goals, while experiencing tremendous growth in its membership. McNeill herself left her corporate job to start a construction company, which she has parlayed into a small dynasty as president of MCO Construction & Services, Inc., MCO Consulting, Inc., Constructively Speaking, Inc. Colbert/Ball Tax Franchise, Speak 2 Share, Inc. and the International MasterMind Association, Inc. - which has produced several authors such Dr. Mia Y. Merritt and a host of successful entrepreneurs.

The *MasterMind Women's Group* has seen members come and go, but the nucleus and precepts on which it was founded have remained. In 2005, the group restructured and the *MasterMind Empowerment Association* was born, and as the organization was incorporated for the first time it saw an influx in membership, growing to nearly one hundred members. For the first time the membership included men and children. It was also at this time that the organization's annual meeting began to be restructured into the conference that it has become today.

Once again in 2007 the organization began to remake itself, changing its name from *MasterMind Empowerment Association, Inc.* to the *International MasterMind Association, Inc.* to encompass the membership that has now spread from the United States to the Caribbean.

And he hath put a new song in my mouth
Psalm 40:3

STEPS TOWARD MASTERMINDING

Name:: _____   Phone: _____   Email: _____

SURVEY: A PERSONAL ASSESSMENT

THE FUNDAMENTALS OF THE SURVEY

The survey is completed at the beginning of each year. The survey will assist you in setting your goals for the year. It is beneficial to complete the survey prior to setting your goals each year.

The survey is to be completed and included in your report. Completing the survey before writing your goals helps you define goals in each area of your life. This is because the survey gives you an overview of where balance is needed. If you notice a lot of "no's" in the area of health, then you know you are out of balance in that area and need to set goals in order to achieve stability, and continued growth and happiness.

THE TEN AREAS OF YOUR LIFE

Remember the annual survey is the starting point to help you grow and reflect on important areas of your life. Be truthful and upfront with yourself.

1. SPIRITUAL
Humans are triune beings. The three parts of our being are body, mind and spirit. To become balanced individuals we must not neglect our spirits

2. FAMILY
Family is an area sometimes overlooked or not thought of at all. This normally happens because in our minds we take for granted that by default they are automatically first. It is important that we have very definitive family goals and aspirations.

3. FINANCIAL
A great deal of the stress that a lot of us encounter is because of mismanagement of finances. This exercise helps us to place everything in our lives into perspective.

4. HEALTH
We have only one body and when it is ruined that is it. We do not get another one. So it would be in our best interest to take care of our bodies.

5. EDUCATIONAL
Knowledge is power and we are on an eternal quest for knowledge. Acquiring knowledge is how we grow as individuals.

6. PERSONAL DEVELOPMENT
Personal goals are set to remind us that we have to invest time in ourselves.

7. BUSINESS/CAREER
In your business or career, you should have definite goals. The setting and achieving of these goals can be the measure of your growth in business or your career.

8. RECREATIONAL
Many times we let the other areas of our lives crowd in on us, and we forget to take a moment to enjoy life. Sometimes we need a recess from our lives, a moment to just laugh, have fun and live.

9. CIVIC
This is relative to your community involvement. As citizens we all have an obligation to give back to others what we have learned so that we can help fuel the next generation.

10. CREATIVITY
We all have innate creative qualities which are often revealed in subjects that capture our interest. For many, creativity comes naturally and is hard to deny. For others, self discovery, reflections, or perhaps a classroom setting may be utilized to reveal and fine tune hidden talents.

SURVEY: A PERSONAL ASSESSMENT

SPIRITUAL

	DATE		DATE		DATE		COMMENTS / NOTES
	YES	NO	YES	NO	YES	NO	
Do you read your Bible daily/weekly?							
Do you give to worthwhile causes?							
Do you attend services to receive spiritual growth?							
Is your spiritual life balanced?							
Do you include your family in your spiritual plans?							
Do you do something to make this world a better place spiritually?							
Have you planned your faith period?							
Do you meditate?							
Do you believe in a Creator?							
Are you helping others?							

FAMILY

	DATE		DATE		DATE		COMMENTS / NOTES
	YES	NO	YES	NO	YES	NO	
Do you have a Family Mission Statement?							
Do you have Family Time (monthly/weekly)?							
Do you make time to spend with your siblings?							
Are all family members insured?							
Are you helping family members to set goals and make plans?							

A PERSONAL ASSESSMENT

FINANCIAL

	DATE			DATE			DATE			COMMENTS / NOTES
	YES	NO		YES	NO		YES	NO		
How much money do you want? $_____										
Are you current in filing your taxes?										
Do you know how much money you need to retire?										
Have you maxed out your 401K?										
Have you maxed out your Tax Shelter Annuity?										
if Self-Employed have you maxed out your SEP/Single K?										
Have you maxed out your Individual Retirement Account?										
Have you maxed out your Roth IRA?										
Do you have Long-term savings?										
Do you have Short-term savings?										
Do you invest in stocks?										
DRIPS (Dividend Reinvestment Plan)?										
Do You have Car Insurance?										
Do You have Homeowners' Insurance?										
Do You have Life Insurance on self and family members?										
Do you have Disability Insurance?										
Do you have Long Term Care Insurance?										
Do you have an updated Will?										
Do you utilize a Trust in your estate plan?										
Does your family know where you keep important papers?										
Are you a member of Better Investing?										
Have you checked your credit score this year?										
Are you a homeowner?										
Do you own Investment property?										

11

SURVEY: A PERSONAL ASSESSMENT

HEALTH

	DATE	YES	NO	DATE	YES	NO	DATE	YES	NO	COMMENTS / NOTES
Have you had a:										
WOMEN: Annual PAP Exam?										
MEN: Prostate Exam?										
GENERAL HEALTH (Have you received these exams?)										
Colonic exam?										
Eye exam?										
Dental exam/ dental cleaning twice yearly?										
Breast exam?										
Colonoscopy?										
Heart Disease exam?										
Bone Density exam?										
Podiatry?										
Do you have a Primary Care Physician?										
Do you have health insurance?										

EDUCATION

	DATE	YES	NO	DATE	YES	NO	DATE	YES	NO	COMMENTS / NOTES
Continued Education?										
No. of books Read Annually?										
Are your children going to college?										
Do you have a daily time to study?										
Will you share your knowledge with others?										
Do you possess education balance?										
Are you going to achieve great wisdom?										

12

SURVEY: A PERSONAL ASSESSMENT

PERSONAL DEVELOPMENT

	DATE			DATE			DATE			COMMENTS / NOTES
	YES	NO		YES	NO		YES	NO		
Do you have a specific activity for Personal Development?										
Do you set goals for:										
6 months?										
1 year?										
5 years?										
10 years?										
29 years?										

BUSINESS & CAREER

	DATE			DATE			DATE			COMMENTS / NOTES
	YES	NO		YES	NO		YES	NO		
Do you own a business?										
Do you have a business plan of action?										
Do you have a financial plan/forecast for your business?										
Do you have prearranged plan to sell/liquidate business at your:										
Death?										
Disability?										
Retirement?										
Are key people insured in the event of death or disability?										
Have you paid quarterly taxes (941)?										
Is your employee compensation package competitive?										
Have you set up a Dun & Bradstreet # for your business?										
Do you set regular appointments to market your business?										

SURVEY: A PERSONAL ASSESSMENT

RECREATION

	DATE		DATE		DATE		COMMENTS / NOTES
	YES	NO	YES	NO	YES	NO	
Do you travel for fun and recreation?							
Do you take a vacation?							
Do you have a personal fitness program?							
Do you plan time for family recreation?							
Are you living a recreationally balanced life?							
Do you plan to take time off for yourself?							

CIVIC (ASSOCIATIONS)

	DATE		DATE		DATE		COMMENTS / NOTES
	YES	NO	YES	NO	YES	NO	
Are you a member of any Professional Organizations?							
Are you a member of any Spiritual Organizations?							
Are you a member of any Volunteer/Non-Profit Organizations?							
Are you a member of any Social Organizations?							

CREATIVITY

	DATE		DATE		DATE		COMMENTS / NOTES
	YES	NO	YES	NO	YES	NO	
Do you have a hobby or collect and display items?							
Do you have a talent and an opportunity to share it with others?							
Are you inspired by art and exhibits?							
Have you ever thought of writing a book?							

Writing Your Affirmation

The first step in the MasterMind plan is to write your affirmation. Your affirmation does not reflect your current situation, but what you expect your situation to be by faith and planning.

Remember to be very specific. You are **AFFIRMING**, thereby making an **AFFIRMATION.** When writing your affirmation write down whom you are as a child in Christ, heir of the kingdom. Writing an affirmation is a worthwhile undertaking that cannot be completed in a day or two. However, when it is finished, you will be extremely proud of what you have written about yourself. You will have defined who you are after much self-analysis.

Your affirmation should become a part of your daily routine. Say it out loud at least twice per day. Once you do this you will begin to conform to what you speak, and in time your circumstances will begin to change to what you proclaim through your affirmation. Still you must remember that dreams and desires only become a reality if we work on them. Merely saying them is not enough.

You should include in your affirmation every area of your life, as it is your goal to create balance in your life. The content of the affirmation should be written in the present tense and not the future tense. Make several copies of your affirmation to post in areas that you frequent like your refrigerator or bathroom mirror. You can review sample affirmations in the Appendices, which may help you in writing your own affirmation.

Write a draft of your affirmation. Read through it and make any changes, when you are ready write your affirmation on the following page, then sign and date. Make as many copies as you need.

NOTES:

_____
_____
_____
_____
_____
_____
_____
_____
_____
_____
_____
_____
_____
_____
_____
_____
_____
_____
_____
_____
_____
_____
_____
_____
_____
_____
_____
_____
_____
_____
_____
_____

Sample Affirmation

I WILL ARRIVE EARLY FOR EACH APPOINTMENT, NOT JUST ON TIME AND DAILY ASK THE QUESTION- WHAT WOULD JESUS DO?

Faith without works is dead and works without faith is dead; therefore I will work like it all depends on me and pray with faith like it all depends on God. God is making me into the very best person with honesty, integrity, frugality, and charity, while in abundance. He has chosen for me this day happiness, success, right action, peace, love and good will for all today. My purpose is to praise God with my life and my desire is to do His will. I will serve God by serving others and for God to bless me to be a blessing.

Spiritually: I will pray, meditate, read and study from 4:00am - 5:45am daily and pray for God's divine will in my life. I will pay tithe and offering of 20% of income, witness about Christ's blessing daily and invite one person to Bible study weekly. My prayer is for a humbling spirit and removing the word "I" from my conversation.

Family: My husband is the most important person in my life, and my desire is to express this through my actions. I will help my children experience greater joys and ensure that they are reading and studying God's word. I will encourage each to read a Proverb a day. We will discuss and plan different family activities. Weekly, I will prepare healthy meals for my family.

Financially: I will have in my possession $15,000.00 a month passive income by December 31st, XXXX, which will come to me in various amounts from time to time during the interim. In return for this money I will give the most efficient service of which I am capable. I will render the fullest possible quantity and the best possible quality of service in the capacity of a businessperson. I believe that I will have this money in my possession. My faith is so strong that I can now see this money before my eyes. I can touch it with my hands. It is now awaiting transfer to me at this time and in the proportion that I deliver the service I intend to render. I am awaiting a plan by which to accumulate this money, and will follow that plan when it is received. In addition, I will save 10%, invest 20%, and tithe 20% of my income by December 31st, XXXX.

Health: Daily I will reduce the amount of bleached foods, consume vitamins, drink 64 ounces of water, perform stretch exercises, and eat a healthy diet. I will read in the health materials weekly and dress the best daily. I will detoxify my system regularly.

Educationally: I will build my English vocabulary, learn Spanish, and Black history. I will read two books and listen to two audio recordings a month while learning more about technology.

Business: I will build my businesses to the glory of God by giving Him all praise for His perfect work. I pray that God increases my wisdom, knowledge, understanding, profitability, and productivity in all areas of my life. I will begin earlier and end earlier by setting at least ten early appointments weekly to market and check my projects and businesses daily. I will plan and execute a succession plan and an exit strategy for retirement. I am partially retired and I will totally retire by December 31st, XXXX.

Civic: Each week I will perform at least one task in two civic areas of my life and invite one new person each month to MasterMind

Recreational: I will Plan an activity for recreation monthly.

Personal: I will develop a personal development program. I am more conscious of my language.

Your Affirmation

_____

_____

_____

_____

_____

_____

_____

_____

_____

_____

_____

_____

_____

_____

_____

_____

_____

_____

_____

_____

_____

_____

_____

_____

_____

_____

_____

Sign: _____ Date:_____

NOTES:

_____

_____

_____

_____

_____

_____

_____

_____

_____

_____

_____

_____

_____

_____

_____

_____

_____

_____

_____

_____

_____

_____

_____

_____

_____

_____

_____

_____

_____

Ten Steps to Goal Setting

There are ten areas in which to set goals; however, you may choose some areas or all of the areas. This is up to you. Once again MasterMind promotes balance. This is why we encourage you to set goals in all ten areas.

You must not just set goals, though. You must also devise an action plan for accomplishing each goal you have made. You may set a financial goal of saving $50.00 per week. Your action plan to accomplish this goal could be to have the money automatically debited from your checking account and credited to your savings account. At the end of the week you should evaluate your goals and action plans and see what progress you have made.

Spiritual Goals

Humans are triune beings. The three parts of our being are body, mind and spirit. The most neglected of the three is probably our spirits. Usually we correlate spirit with "religion", which can be a major factor in nurturing our spirit, but not necessarily. To become balanced individuals, we must not neglect our spirits; That is why MasterMind encourages you to set spiritual goals. An example of a spiritual goal may be to meditate daily.

Personal Goals

Personal goals are set to remind us that we have to invest time in ourselves. An example of a personal goal may be to go to the spa once a month.

Health Goals

We have only one body and when it is ruined that is it. We do not get another one. So it would be in your best interest to take care of your body. An example of a health goal would be to quit smoking.

You should consider some of these questions when setting health goals:
- What do I want to accomplish in my lifetime?
- What am I willing to do to keep myself fit and healthy for God's work?
- Will I eat the proper foods to give me energy and vitality?
- Will I educate myself on my body and what makes it function?
- Will I cut out the foods that are harmful to my system?
- Will I exercise daily?

Educational Goals

Knowledge is power and we are on an eternal quest for knowledge. Acquiring knowledge is how we grow as individuals. Every living thing grows - spiritually, mentally and physically. Educational goals should not be confided to classroom learning, but should encompass every facet of learning. An example of an educational goal may be to learn how to design a website.

Financial Goals

A great deal of the stress that a lot of us encounter is because of mismanagement of finances. Having a plan for your finances can prevent a lot of that mismanagement and in turn elevate some stress in your life. When making your financial goals you should consider your long term economic future. These goals should include a plan for your family should something happen to you. We do not often think of these things until we are faced with the situation. This exercise helps us to place everything in our lives into perspective. An example of a financial goal can be to set a monthly budget.

Business/Career Goals

In your business or career you should have definite goals. The setting and achieving of these goals can be the measure of your growth in business or your career.

These goals are very important as they determine the service that you will render in order to obtain your financial goals. Once you are ready to determine what it is that you like to do, and decide that you would like to earn money doing it, you put your action plan into place. An example of a business goal is to make $1,000,000.00 in sales. A career goal could be to get a promotion.

Family Goals

Goals in the area of family are sometimes overlooked or not thought of at all. This normally happens because in our minds we take for granted that by default they are automatically first. It is important that we have very definitive family goals and aspirations. This exercise does several things. It causes families to spend more time together. It also helps the family move in one direction that ensures generational prosperity. Strong families are born from strong family values.

Recreational Goals

This area may not seem important. Sometimes we let the other areas of our lives crowd in on us, and we forget to take a moment to enjoy life. Sometimes we need a recess from our lives, a moment to just laugh, have fun, and live. A recreational goal could be to take a Mediterranean Cruise.

Civic Goals

Civic goals are relative to your community involvement. As citizens, we all have an obligation to give back to others what we have learned so that we can help fuel the next generation. Donate your time and talent with organizations that you like. You may chose organizations like high schools, colleges, faith based organizations or medial research organizations. A civic goal may be to volunteer four hours per month at a local high school.

Creative Goals

We all have innate creative qualities which are often revealed in subjects that capture our interest. For many, creativity comes naturally and is hard to deny. For others, self discovery, reflection, or perhaps a classroom setting may be utilized to reveal and fine tune hidden talents.

Of course God is the ultimate creator and source of our creative abilities. From the ever changing seasonal landscapes to artful ideas born from selections chosen to beautify architectural designs, creativity appears in limitless ways. For example, someone may use creativity verbally to motivate an unhappy child or fire up a corporate seminar, while someone else may show creativity through the selection of wardrobe ensembles or meal presentations.

NOTES:

_____
_____
_____
_____
_____
_____
_____
_____
_____
_____
_____
_____
_____
_____
_____
_____
_____
_____
_____
_____
_____
_____
_____
_____
_____
_____
_____
_____
_____
_____

How to Set and Write Effective Goals

Ultimate Focus: Six Steps to Goal Setting Success

What is a "DreamLine?" It is a dream with targeted date of completion, okay, a goal if you will....If you are tired of the word "goal" then use "DreamLine."

SAMPLE HEALTH GOAL:
  • I do something everyday to help me be healthy and strong.

Once you establish you goal, come up with an action plan to meet the goal.

For example:
  • Every day at 7am I ride my bike for 20 minutes.

For the highest degree of success, ease in following through and accountability _goal statements should meet the following criteria:_

1. **SIMPLY STATED:** This is not a memo. Keep it brief and you own it. It is easy to memorize and repeat.

2. **POSITIVE**. Use contrast if you have trouble deciding what you want. State what you don't want and flip it.

3. **PRESENT TENSE**. Believe it is yours now.

4. **BELIEVABLE** (to you). Whatever fits, works for YOU.

5. **MEASURABLE.** Make sure your goal AND your plans to reach your goal(s) are measurable. If you said, "I am going to start riding my bike," will you? You probably will not because there is no accountability or measurability.   But if it is seven in the morning, where are you for 20 minutes? It is the measurability that makes it believable. Again, it must be measurable. If not, how will you know when you achieve your goal?!

6. **HAVE REWARDS.** Most of us leave this out. Why do we have this goal? WHAT is the benefit? In this person's case the benefit of achieving the goal is "to be healthy and strong".

More Goal Samples:

Financial: I maintain a college fund for my child.

Spiritual: I keep daily meditation time with the Lord.

Making An Action Plan

A goal without a plan is nothing more than wishful thinking. For this reason a major part of MasterMind is creating an action plan for your goals. MasterMind members are encouraged to devise an action plan for each goal they set.

Your action plan can be defined as your method for achieving your goals. For example if you set a health goal of losing ten pounds within six months, the action plan could be to exercise daily for one hour from 5:00 am - 6:00 am; or walk for twenty minutes before and after work.

The Bible says that faith without works is dead. So we must work daily toward achieving these goals.

NOTES:

_____
_____
_____
_____
_____
_____
_____
_____
_____
_____
_____
_____
_____
_____
_____
_____
_____
_____
_____
_____
_____
_____
_____
_____
_____
_____
_____
_____
_____
_____
_____
_____

Think & Grow Rich Questionnaire

The following questionnaire was taken from Napoleon Hill's *Think & Grow Rich*. Completing this form is imperative to beginning your MasterMind journey. It will help you to begin to determine which goals you need to set.

1. Fix in your mind the exact amount of money you desire. It is not sufficient merely to say, "I want plenty of money". Be definite as to the amount. (There is a psychological reason for definiteness, which is described in *Think & Grow Rich*.)

_____

_____

_____

_____

_____

_____

2. Determine exactly what you intend to give in return for the money you desire. (There is no such reality as "something for nothing.)

_____

_____

_____

_____

_____

_____

3. Establish a definite date when you intend to possess the money you desire.

_____

_____

_____

_____

_____

_____

4. Create a definite plan for carrying out your desire, and being at once, whether you are ready or not, to put this plan into action.

_____

_____

_____

_____

_____

_____

5. Write our a clear, concise statement of the amount of money you intend to acquire, name the time limit for its acquisition, state what you intend to give in return for the money, and describe clearly the plan through which you intend to accumulate it.

_____

_____

_____

_____

_____

_____

6. Read your written statement aloud, twice daily, once just before retiring at night, and once after arising in the morning. As you read, see, feel and believe yourself already in possession of the money..

_____

_____

_____

_____

_____

_____

Sample Income Circles

Another tool to help in setting goals is the Income Circles. The Income Circles are specifically directed at financial goals. At the center of the page you would put yourself, and branching out from you would be the sources of income you would like to attract to yourself.

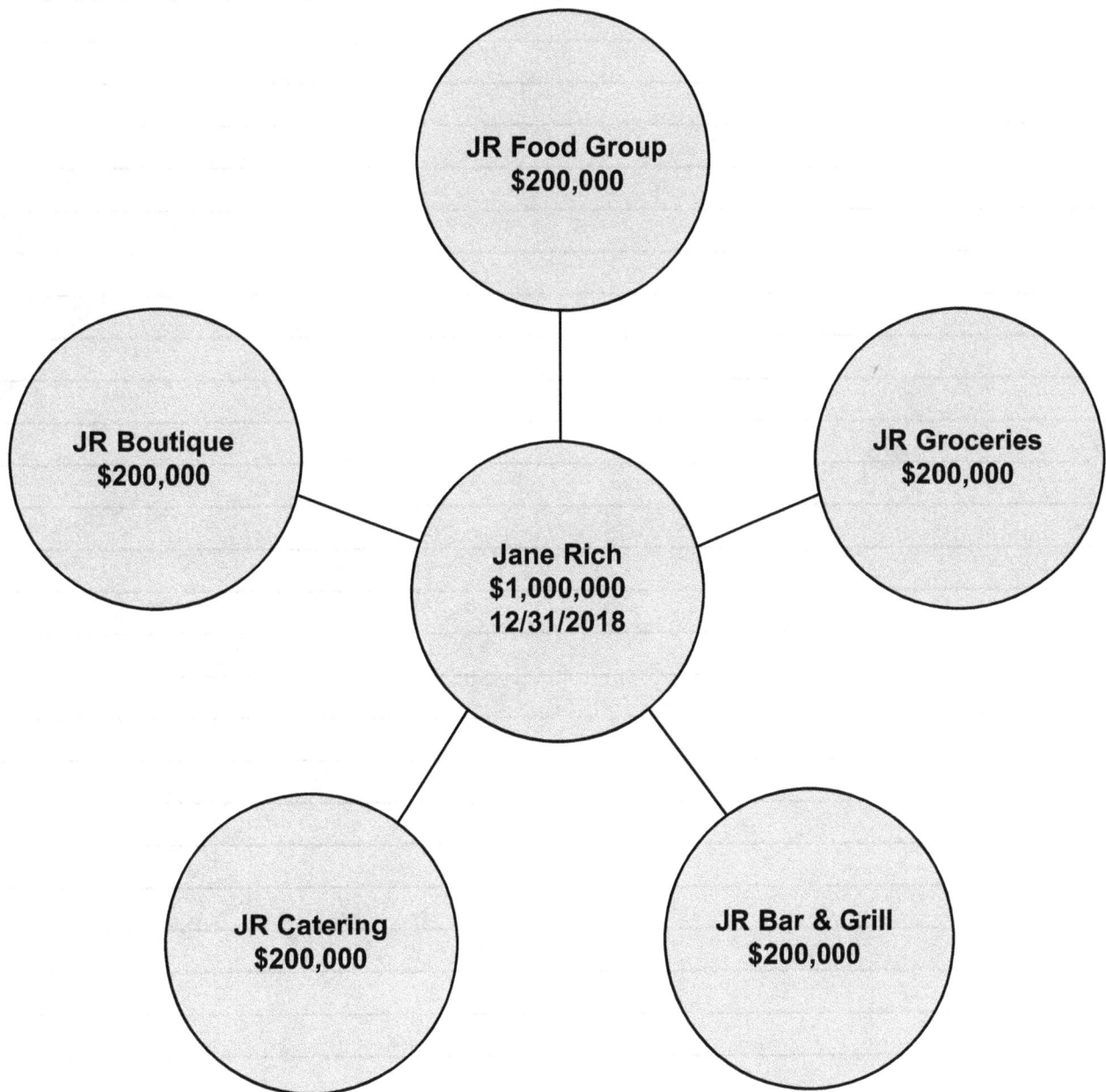

JR Food Group
$200,000

JR Boutique
$200,000

JR Groceries
$200,000

Jane Rich
$1,000,000
12/31/2018

JR Catering
$200,000

JR Bar & Grill
$200,000

NOTES:

_____
_____
_____
_____
_____
_____
_____
_____
_____
_____
_____
_____
_____
_____
_____
_____
_____
_____
_____
_____
_____
_____
_____
_____
_____
_____
_____
_____

Your Income Circles

Go ahead and write your income circles on this page.

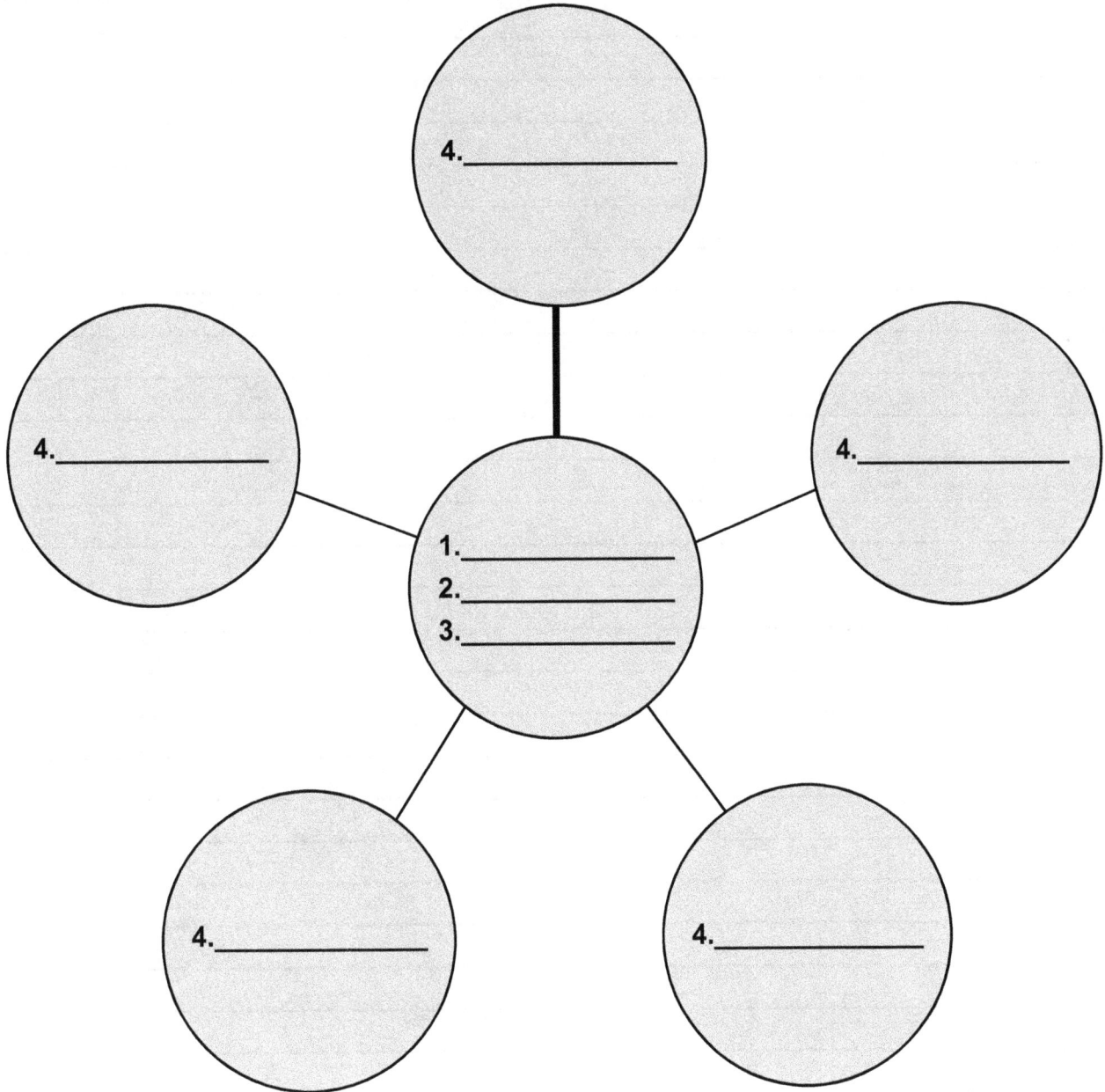

4._____

4._____

4._____

1._____
2._____
3._____

4._____

4._____

NOTES:

_____

_____

_____

_____

_____

_____

_____

_____

_____

_____

_____

_____

_____

_____

_____

_____

_____

_____

_____

_____

_____

_____

_____

_____

_____

Your Obituary

Writing your obituary may seem like a very morbid task, but writing your obituary will assist you in putting your goals into prospective.

Sample Obituary:

Amy Elizabeth Jones was granted her angel wings on March 6th 2005. Her final days were spent surrounded by family and friends that Amy had touched in some small way throughout her short, yet very memorable life.

Amy's life would seem too short to many, but those of us who were touched by her understood that the quality of existence far exceeds the quantity of time in which one lives. Her gentle smile, tiny fingers and baby soft skin brought so much joy to our family.

Although she was so tiny and frail, she gave us all such courage and hope and reminded us of the preciousness of life. She loved to rock and swing. She could spend hours rocking in her favorite chair while cuddling close to those she loved so much. She enjoyed music and reading stories.

Amy is survived by her loving parents, Craig and Amy Jones of Rutland Vermont; sister Katie Jones; paternal grandparents Bob and Margaret Jones; uncle Mark Jones of Raleigh, NC.

In lieu of flowers, donations may be made to:

NOTES:

_____

_____

_____

_____

_____

_____

_____

_____

_____

_____

_____

_____

_____

_____

_____

_____

_____

_____

_____

_____

_____

_____

_____

_____

_____

_____

_____

_____

_____

_____

_____

Writing Your Obituary

Guideline Instructions

Name: _____

Born: _____

To Parents: _____

City of Residence: _____

Education: _____

_____

_____

Employment: _____

_____

_____

_____

_____

_____

_____

_____

Civic and Community Involvement: _____

_____

_____

_____

Survivors: _____

_____

_____

_____

NOTES:

Sample Annual/Midyear Report

Jane Doe James
2002 Annual Report
One Year Goals

Spiritual

1. Pray Daily

2. Read Bible Daily

3. Attend Church Weekly

4. Tithe 10% of income

5. Tithe of my time

Family

1. Spend a minimum of one hour of quality time daily with children

2. Family prayer time daily

3. QT with husband weekly

Financial

1. Save 10% of salary

2. Raise credit score

3. Fund IRA

Health

1. Get yearly physical

2. Get yearly mammogram

3. Exercise daily

Health (cont'd)

4. Eliminate Sugar from diet

5. Drink water daily

Educational

1. Pass GRE Exam

2. Take French Classes

Personal

1. Journal Daily

2. Alone Time Weekly

3. Visit Salon bi-weekly

Business/Career

1. Complete Business Plan

2. Find investor for business

3. Get website functional

Recreational

1. Vacation to Europe

2. Go out once a quarter with girlfriends

Civic

1. Attend MasterMind meetings weekly

2. Volunteer with library

Creative

1. Paint Daily

2. Brainstorm Weekly

Your Annual/Midyear Report

Name:_____

From:_____ To:_____ Date Completed:_____

Spiritual Goals:_____
_____
_____
_____
_____

Action Plan:_____
_____
_____

Family Goals: _____
_____
_____
_____
_____

Action Plan:_____
_____
_____

Financial Goals:_____
_____
_____
_____
_____

Action Plan:_____
_____

Financial Goals (cont'd):_____

_____

Health Goals: _____

_____

_____

_____

_____

Action Plan:_____

_____

_____

Educational Goals:_____

_____

_____

_____

_____

Action Plan:_____

_____

_____

Personal Goals: _____

_____

_____

_____

_____

Action Plan:_____

_____

_____

Business/Career Goals: _____
_____
_____
_____
_____
_____

Action Plan:_____
_____
_____

Recreational Goals: _____
_____
_____
_____
_____

Action Plan:_____
_____
_____

Civic Goals: _____
_____
_____
_____
_____

Action Plan:_____
_____
_____

Creative Goals: _____
_____
_____
_____
_____
_____

Action Plan: _____
_____
_____

Weekly MasterMind Plan

Dreams Do Come True

" 'Remember the Lord thy God: for it is He that giveth thee power to get wealth'. That power begins with being open and obedient to valuable information that is presented to you."

T.D. Jakes

I started with the MasterMind Group in 1997. Ann McNeill saw me in church and told me to go and purchase a book I had never heard of called *"Think and Grow Rich"* by Napoleon Hill. For about two months every time she spoke with me in church she would ask me, "Did you get the book?". And I reluctantly would say, "No". After being embarrassed because she was very persistent in her wanting me to read this book, I went and purchased the book and began to read it. I think I purchased the book because I didn't want her to think that I was crazy, because I promised her time and time again that I would get this book. Well, I began to read this book and began to read information that I had never heard before. I became very interested in this book because I had always believed that I was supposed to be successful but just couldn't quite put my hands on the "it" that would walk me through the process. This book answered a lot of my questions. I began to tell other people about this book and they too had the same revelation. At this point I began to change my thought process.

After I told Ann that I had the book, Ann invited me to meeting at her home she affectionately calls "the house of faith!" The house was located in a beautiful neighborhood in Miami Lakes, Florida. It was a gorgeous house with huge rooms in it, a swimming pool overlooking the kitchen area with a fireplace in the sitting room. She even had a guest quarters and a tennis court. The property was located in front of the golf course. I said to myself, what ever she's doing, I want to know so I can live like this! I went to this meeting one Saturday morning at 8:00am and was greeted by other women with warm smiles and there was an excitement in the air. Not only was Ann successful, but also these other women owned their own businesses and were also successful. At this meeting, I was introduced to a system that was talked about in the book *"Think and Grow Rich"* that I was reading. The system is goal setting, which includes a weekly meeting to monitor your success in meeting these goals. I was told to write goals in every area of my life because I needed to have balance in my life. I was also told to write an affirmation of the person I wanted to become. These goals would include the type of spiritual life I wanted to have, the kind of money I wanted to make, the kind of business I wanted to own, the kind of education I wanted to accomplish, how I planned to get involved with civic activities to help my community, setting goals to spend quality time with family, the kind of health I wanted to be in, and the personal goals that I set for myself to accomplish. At first, I thought it all sounded like hog wash but I continued to come to the meetings because I could see results in the goals I made for myself from week to week. Also, as I was setting these goals, I noticed that I became a magnet for the goals that I set. For instance, if I wanted to get a contract for a certain amount, I would mysteriously get a call from someone asking me to work on special events or plan programs, etc. They wanted to pay me for the things that I would normally do for free! This began to become so exciting to me until I became bold and began to set bigger goals. I can remember a time when I would tell everyone how I was going to drive my Lexus Sports Coupe. The Lexus just came out and I didn't have the money to afford one at the time but I knew I wanted that car. I went and test drove the car and continued to tell people that that was going to be my next car. Well, a year or two later I got my Lexus Sports Coupe and everyone in may church and family knew I said I was going to get this car. They became so excited for me. Many of them could not believe it! This was just the beginning of what this system of setting and monitoring goals and speaking things into existence has done in my life. I began to work on myself mentally by reading the Word of God and reading positive books on every area that I set a goal in. This increased my knowledge and allowed me to grow beyond my wildest dreams each of these areas.

Now let's fast forward this story to 2007, I always said that in the financial areas of my goals that I wanted to receive a certain amount of money in increments from different sources/streams monthly. I can honestly say that monthly I receive checks from 5 sources and the amounts are growing daily. I know that my money grew because I grew in the area of money. I don't want you to think that this is just about material gain; however, money is important even though people don't want to admit it at times. I have become a new person mentally, financially and spiritually. I am now the Director of 3 church choirs, and in charge of more than 30 people on the Praise Team for a Mega church. I'm a consultant for various churches in the area of music and I give advice to ministers on how they could develop their music ministries. I have seen the change in my life and so has many other people seen the hand of God on my life. I constantly get encouragement and applauses on how my life has changed, even when I'm going through trials/challenges/test. I don't give up or give in, I continue through the hard times because I understand spiritual/universal laws. I am a believer of reaping and sowing. Therefore, I try extremely hard to do my part and sow only the seed that I want to grow and manifest in my life. My most recent accomplishment is that I'm with a 4 Billion dollar MLM company and have over 200 business partners whom I train and assist in accomplishing their goals. The most exciting part of this is that in order for me to achieve my goals, I have to make sure other business partners get their goals accomplished first. This brings me joy that I can set a goal to help other people meet their goal and by default I get my goal accomplished. The focus is not on me, it's on others and I love that.

In closing, I would like to encourage everyone to write a vision for their life. Some people call it an affirmation but I call it a vision. Who do you really want to become without any restraints, doubts or fears? Once you figure out who you want to become, you can began the road to setting up a blueprint for your life that would get you to your final destination, success! You must have faith, patience and endurance. You must speak a language that will get you the results you want and erase any negative thoughts or fears that will cripple you and stop you from meeting your goal. You have to decide in your mind that you are going to be successful regardless of where you were born, the color of your skin or the educational background you may have. You have to stop making excuses and change whatever you're doing in your life that is not giving you the results you want and perhaps find a successful person that could support/mentor you into the person you want to become. Also remember that everyone is going to have a success story and before you become a master you may be a disaster! Just keep going and don't stop. Learn from your failures and don't let your failures cripple you. Every successful person had pitfalls and stumbling blocks, but they didn't let that stop them because the race is not given to the swift or the strong; but to the one that endures until the end. You have to change your mindset into a healthy one. Look at Donald Trump, he lost all of his money at one time but because he had a mindset to succeed, he came back and made more money within a few years. You have to dream big and don't let your present situation block you from your success. Increase your goals yearly. Don't become complacent with doing a good job when you can do a great job. You have to continually work on yourself by developing your mind and your actions. John Maxwell says "the secret to your future is hidden in your daily routine; you will never change your life, until you change something that you do daily." The important thing is to be able at any moments notice to sacrifice what we are for what we could become! It is safe to say that the MasterMind Women's Group has given me the tools I needed to change my world. The information and books we read opens my mind and allows me to go to new heights. My goal/mission is to start a Junior MIA (Millionaires in Action) Group with a group of young ladies that I will be mentoring in 2008. I want to give them the opportunity of showing them the system of seeing goals and reading mind changing literature that will literally change their life while they are young.

Gail Seay

NOTES:

_____
_____
_____
_____
_____
_____
_____
_____
_____
_____
_____
_____
_____
_____
_____
_____
_____
_____
_____
_____
_____
_____
_____
_____
_____
_____
_____
_____
_____

Monthly Goals

Month_____

SPIRITUAL:

Reading:_____ Author:_____ Date Completion / %:_____

	GOALS	Completion Date
1.	_____	_____
2.	_____	_____
3.	_____	_____

FAMILY:

Reading:_____ Author:_____ Date Completion / %:_____

	GOALS	Completion Date
1.	_____	_____
2.	_____	_____
3.	_____	_____

FINANCIAL:

Reading:_____ Author:_____ Date Completion / %:_____

	GOALS	Completion Date
1.	_____	_____
2.	_____	_____
3.	_____	_____

HEALTH:

Reading:_____ Author:_____ Date Completion / %:_____

	GOALS	Completion Date
1.	_____	_____
2.	_____	_____
3.	_____	_____

EDUCATIONAL:

Reading:_____ Author:_____ Date Completion / %:_____

GOALS **Completion Date**

1. _____ _____
2. _____ _____
3. _____ _____

PERSONAL DEVELOPMENT:

Reading:_____ Author:_____ Date Completion / %:_____

GOALS **Completion Date**

1. _____ _____
2. _____ _____
3. _____ _____

BUSINESS/CAREER:

Reading:_____ Author:_____ Date Completion / %:_____

GOALS **Completion Date**

1. _____ _____
2. _____ _____
3. _____ _____

RECREATIONAL:

Reading:_____ Author:_____ Date Completion / %:_____

GOALS **Completion Date**

1. _____ _____
2. _____ _____
3. _____ _____

CIVIC:

Reading:_____ Author:_____ Date Completion / %:_____

GOALS   **Completion Date**

1. _____   _____

2. _____   _____

3. _____   _____

CREATIVITY:

Reading:_____ Author:_____ Date Completion / %:_____

GOALS   **Completion Date**

1. _____   _____

2. _____   _____

3. _____   _____

Notes:

WEEKLY MASTERMIND PLAN

NAME: _____

FOR WEEK OF: _____

MEMORY SCRIPTURE or QUOTE FOR THE MONTH:

SPIRITUAL GOALS:	Accomplished

Book:		Pgs.	Projected		Pgs.	Actual							
SPIRITUAL GOALS ACTION PLAN:					M	T	W	T	F	S	S	%	

FAMILY GOALS:		**Accomplished**

Book:		Pgs.	Projected		Pgs.	Actual

FAMILY GOALS ACTION PLAN:	M	T	W	T	F	S	S	%

FINANCIAL GOALS:		**Accomplished**

Book:		Pgs.	Projected		Pgs.	Actual

FINANCIAL GOALS ACTION PLAN:	M	T	W	T	F	S	S	%

HEALTH GOALS:					Accomplished				

Book:	Pgs.	Projected		Pgs.	Actual

HEALTH GOALS ACTION PLAN:	M	T	W	T	F	S	S	%

EDUCATIONAL GOALS:					Accomplished				

Book:	Pgs.	Projected		Pgs.	Actual

EDUCATIONAL GOALS ACTION PLAN:	M	T	W	T	F	S	S	%

PERSONAL GOALS:					Accomplished			

Book:		Pgs.	Projected		Pgs.	Actual		

PERSONAL GOALS ACTION PLAN:	M	T	W	T	F	S	S	%

BUSINESS/CAREER GOALS:					Accomplished			

Book:		Pgs.	Projected		Pgs.	Actual		

BUSINESS/CAREER GOALS ACTION PLAN:	M	T	W	T	F	S	S	%

RECREATIONAL GOALS:		**Accomplished**

Book:	Pgs.	Projected		Pgs.	Actual

RECREATIONAL GOALS ACTION PLAN:	M	T	W	T	F	S	S	%

CIVIC GOALS:		**Accomplished**

Book:	Pgs.	Projected		Pgs.	Actual

CIVIC GOALS ACTION PLAN:	M	T	W	T	F	S	S	%

CREATIVITY GOALS:						**Accomplished**				

Book:	Pgs.	Projected		Pgs.	Actual

CREATIVITY GOALS ACTION PLAN:	**M**	**T**	**W**	**T**	**F**	**S**	**S**	**%**

This week's meeting place: _____ Date:_____

Attendees:

1. _____   4._____

2. _____   5._____

3. _____   6._____

Next week's meeting place:_____ Date:_____

Notes:

WEEKLY MASTERMIND PLAN

NAME: _____

FOR WEEK OF: _____

MEMORY SCRIPTURE or QUOTE FOR THE MONTH:

SPIRITUAL GOALS:	Accomplished

Book:		Pgs.	Projected		Pgs.	Actual

SPIRITUAL GOALS ACTION PLAN:	M	T	W	T	F	S	S	%

FAMILY GOALS:		Accomplished

Book:	Pgs.	Projected		Pgs.	Actual

FAMILY GOALS ACTION PLAN:	M	T	W	T	F	S	S	%

FINANCIAL GOALS:		Accomplished

Book:	Pgs.	Projected		Pgs.	Actual

FINANCIAL GOALS ACTION PLAN:	M	T	W	T	F	S	S	%

HEALTH GOALS:					Accomplished				

Book:		Pgs.	Projected		Pgs.	Actual			

HEALTH GOALS ACTION PLAN:	M	T	W	T	F	S	S	%

EDUCATIONAL GOALS:					Accomplished				

Book:		Pgs.	Projected		Pgs.	Actual			

EDUCATIONAL GOALS ACTION PLAN:	M	T	W	T	F	S	S	%

PERSONAL GOALS:							**Accomplished**		
Book:		Pgs.	Projected		Pgs.	Actual			

PERSONAL GOALS ACTION PLAN:	M	T	W	T	F	S	S	%

BUSINESS/CAREER GOALS:							**Accomplished**		
Book:		Pgs.	Projected		Pgs.	Actual			

BUSINESS/CAREER GOALS ACTION PLAN:	M	T	W	T	F	S	S	%

RECREATIONAL GOALS:	Accomplished

Book:		Pgs.	Projected		Pgs.	Actual		

RECREATIONAL GOALS ACTION PLAN:	M	T	W	T	F	S	S	%

CIVIC GOALS:	Accomplished

Book:		Pgs.	Projected		Pgs.	Actual		

CIVIC GOALS ACTION PLAN:	M	T	W	T	F	S	S	%

CREATIVITY GOALS:					**Accomplished**				

Book:		Pgs.	Projected		Pgs.	Actual			

CREATIVITY GOALS ACTION PLAN:	M	T	W	T	F	S	S	%

This week's meeting place: _____ Date:_____

Attendees:

1. _____   4._____

2. _____   5._____

3. _____   6._____

Notes:

WEEKLY MASTERMIND PLAN

NAME: _____

FOR WEEK OF: _____

MEMORY SCRIPTURE or QUOTE FOR THE MONTH:

SPIRITUAL GOALS:							**Accomplished**		

Book:		Pgs.	Projected		Pgs.	Actual			
SPIRITUAL GOALS ACTION PLAN:				**M**	**T**	**W**	**T**	**F**	**S**	**S**	**%**

FAMILY GOALS:		Accomplished

Book:	Pgs.	Projected		Pgs.	Actual

FAMILY GOALS ACTION PLAN:	M	T	W	T	F	S	S	%

FINANCIAL GOALS:		Accomplished

Book:	Pgs.	Projected		Pgs.	Actual

FINANCIAL GOALS ACTION PLAN:	M	T	W	T	F	S	S	%

HEALTH GOALS:									Accomplished		

Book:			Pgs.	Projected		Pgs.	Actual				

HEALTH GOALS ACTION PLAN:	M	T	W	T	F	S	S	%

EDUCATIONAL GOALS:									Accomplished		

Book:			Pgs.	Projected		Pgs.	Actual				

EDUCATIONAL GOALS ACTION PLAN:	M	T	W	T	F	S	S	%

PERSONAL GOALS:						**Accomplished**			

Book:		Pgs.	Projected		Pgs.	Actual			

PERSONAL GOALS ACTION PLAN:	**M**	**T**	**W**	**T**	**F**	**S**	**S**	**%**

BUSINESS/CAREER GOALS:						**Accomplished**			

Book:		Pgs.	Projected		Pgs.	Actual			

BUSINESS/CAREER GOALS ACTION PLAN:	**M**	**T**	**W**	**T**	**F**	**S**	**S**	**%**

RECREATIONAL GOALS:							Accomplished		

Book:		Pgs.	Projected		Pgs.	Actual			

RECREATIONAL GOALS ACTION PLAN:	M	T	W	T	F	S	S	%

CIVIC GOALS:							Accomplished		

Book:		Pgs.	Projected		Pgs.	Actual			

CIVIC GOALS ACTION PLAN:	M	T	W	T	F	S	S	%

CREATIVITY GOALS:		**Accomplished**

Book:		Pgs.	Projected		Pgs.	Actual						

CREATIVITY GOALS ACTION PLAN:	M	T	W	T	F	S	S	%

This week's meeting place: _____ Date: _____

Attendees:

1. _____   4. _____

2. _____   5. _____

3. _____   6. _____

Next week's meeting place: _____ Date: _____

Notes:

WEEKLY MASTERMIND PLAN

NAME: _____

FOR WEEK OF: _____

MEMORY SCRIPTURE or QUOTE FOR THE MONTH:

SPIRITUAL GOALS:	Accomplished

Book:		Pgs.	Projected		Pgs.	Actual						
SPIRITUAL GOALS ACTION PLAN:					**M**	**T**	**W**	**T**	**F**	**S**	**S**	**%**

FAMILY GOALS:			**Accomplished**

Book:		Pgs.	Projected		Pgs.	Actual			

FAMILY GOALS ACTION PLAN:	**M**	**T**	**W**	**T**	**F**	**S**	**S**	**%**

FINANCIAL GOALS:			**Accomplished**

Book:		Pgs.	Projected		Pgs.	Actual			

FINANCIAL GOALS ACTION PLAN:	**M**	**T**	**W**	**T**	**F**	**S**	**S**	**%**

HEALTH GOALS:							Accomplished			

Book:		Pgs.	Projected		Pgs.	Actual				

HEALTH GOALS ACTION PLAN:		**M**	**T**	**W**	**T**	**F**	**S**	**S**	**%**

EDUCATIONAL GOALS:							Accomplished			

Book:		Pgs.	Projected		Pgs.	Actual				

EDUCATIONAL GOALS ACTION PLAN:		**M**	**T**	**W**	**T**	**F**	**S**	**S**	**%**

PERSONAL GOALS:	Accomplished

Book:	Pgs.	Projected		Pgs.	Actual

PERSONAL GOALS ACTION PLAN:	M	T	W	T	F	S	S	%

BUSINESS/CAREER GOALS:	Accomplished

Book:	Pgs.	Projected		Pgs.	Actual

BUSINESS/CAREER GOALS ACTION PLAN:	M	T	W	T	F	S	S	%

RECREATIONAL GOALS:					Accomplished			

Book:	Pgs.	Projected		Pgs.	Actual			

RECREATIONAL GOALS ACTION PLAN:	M	T	W	T	F	S	S	%

CIVIC GOALS:					Accomplished			

Book:	Pgs.	Projected		Pgs.	Actual			

CIVIC GOALS ACTION PLAN:	M	T	W	T	F	S	S	%

CREATIVITY GOALS:								**Accomplished**	

Book:		Pgs.	Projected		Pgs.	Actual			

CREATIVITY GOALS ACTION PLAN:	M	T	W	T	F	S	S	%

This week's meeting place: _____ Date:_____

Attendees:

1. _____   4._____

2. _____   5._____

3. _____   6._____

Next week's meeting place:_____ Date:_____

Notes:

Getting Organized

"No man is a free man until he learns to do his own thinking and gains the courage to act on his own personal initiative." *Napoleon Hill*

I signed up for a conference held on a Saturday in early 2006 called "Women That Win". I had just watched the DVD, "The Secret", and I had been listing, in my mind, all of the things I wanted to manifest for 2006. Yet still I felt disorganized. The conference was well-attended by amazing women, and the panel of speakers shared great ideas for building successful businesses. Two of the speakers mentioned Ann McNeil in their presentations and the last speaker pointed to Ann in the audience and asked her to stand to be recognized. They all praised Ann for her work in creating a MasterMind plan and helping others achieve outstanding results. I had listened to *"Think and Grow Rich"* on CD in my car and I remembered Napoleon Hill's recommendation for starting a MasterMind group. I knew instantly that I wanted to meet Ann and ask her to help me organize a group of like-minded women.

I approached Ann after the conference concluded and introduced myself. She was warm and kind, and agreed to meet with me to discuss creating a MasterMind group in my town. When the day arrived for Ann to come to my house, I could hardly wait. She called and said she was bringing a few of her friends who were also in her MasterMind group. I gathered five women who were as excited as I was about a MasterMind group, and we all sat down with Ann and her extraordinary friends to discuss what to do. I was astounded at their successes in all the different areas of their lives! They were all so balanced, and that made all the difference.
Ann's MasterMind plan was exactly what I needed. It helped me organize my goals for many areas of my life, not just my business. Ann's approach to creating the life you want is perfect for people like me who walk around with an endless list of ideas in their heads, but never seem to organize those thoughts productively. I am eternally grateful to Ann and her friends for sharing their MasterMind system!

Gina Bender

Minding My Own Business

"You don't choose your family. They are God's gift to you, as you are to them."

Desmond Tutu

International MasterMind Association has allowed me to create balance for the first time in my life. It has given me a new pair of eyes to view my life with. Before MasterMind I would work and mother, mother and work. I thought I was successful because of the results in my kids and my profession, but I left myself out of the equation. Everything I did revolved around those two aspects of my life.

I now plan in nine separate areas of life. Areas that I did not even fathom considering before like personal and recreational are now a priority. I read books in all nine areas of my life as well. What MasterMind has done is make me truly live the full life that God has ordained me to live. It helps me measure my growth and learn from my shortcomings. It gives me hope for the future and keeps me focused on my agenda, which discourages others from putting me on theirs. Every year is a new learning experience. I feed off of my other members' goals and achievements. Their insight and wisdom has been fruitful to my life.

Yolanda English

Monthly Goals

Month_____

SPIRITUAL:

Reading:_____ Author:_____ Date Completion / %:_____

	GOALS	Completion Date
1.	_____	_____
2.	_____	_____
3.	_____	_____

FAMILY:

Reading:_____ Author:_____ Date Completion / %:_____

	GOALS	Completion Date
1.	_____	_____
2.	_____	_____
3.	_____	_____

FINANCIAL:

Reading:_____ Author:_____ Date Completion / %:_____

	GOALS	Completion Date
1.	_____	_____
2.	_____	_____
3.	_____	_____

HEALTH:

Reading:_____ Author:_____ Date Completion / %:_____

	GOALS	Completion Date
1.	_____	_____
2.	_____	_____
3.	_____	_____

EDUCATIONAL:

Reading:_____ Author:_____ Date Completion/ %:_____

GOALS   **Completion Date**

1. _____   _____
2. _____   _____
3. _____   _____

PERSONAL DEVELOPMENT:

Reading:_____ Author:_____ Date Completion/ %:_____

GOALS   **Completion Date**

1. _____   _____
2. _____   _____
3. _____   _____

BUSINESS/CAREER:

Reading:_____ Author:_____ Date Completion/ %:_____

GOALS   **Completion Date**

1. _____   _____
2. _____   _____
3. _____   _____

RECREATIONAL:

Reading:_____ Author:_____ Date Completion/ %:_____

GOALS   **Completion Date**

1. _____   _____
2. _____   _____
3. _____   _____

CIVIC:

Reading:_____ Author:_____ Date Completion / %:_____

<table>
<tr><td></td><td>**GOALS**</td><td>**Completion Date**</td></tr>
<tr><td>1.</td><td>_____</td><td>_____</td></tr>
<tr><td>2.</td><td>_____</td><td>_____</td></tr>
<tr><td>3.</td><td>_____</td><td>_____</td></tr>
</table>

CREATIVITY:

Reading:_____ Author:_____ Date Completion / %:_____

<table>
<tr><td></td><td>**GOALS**</td><td>**Completion Date**</td></tr>
<tr><td>1.</td><td>_____</td><td>_____</td></tr>
<tr><td>2.</td><td>_____</td><td>_____</td></tr>
<tr><td>3.</td><td>_____</td><td>_____</td></tr>
</table>

Notes:

WEEKLY MASTERMIND PLAN

NAME: _____

FOR WEEK OF: _____

MEMORY SCRIPTURE or QUOTE FOR THE MONTH:

SPIRITUAL GOALS:	Accomplished

Book:	Pgs.	Projected		Pgs.	Actual

SPIRITUAL GOALS ACTION PLAN:	M	T	W	T	F	S	S	%

FAMILY GOALS:					**Accomplished**		

| Book: | Pgs. | Projected | | Pgs. | Actual |

FAMILY GOALS ACTION PLAN:	M	T	W	T	F	S	S	%

FINANCIAL GOALS:					**Accomplished**		

| Book: | Pgs. | Projected | | Pgs. | Actual |

FINANCIAL GOALS ACTION PLAN:	M	T	W	T	F	S	S	%

HEALTH GOALS:					Accomplished		

Book:		Pgs.	Projected		Pgs.	Actual	

HEALTH GOALS ACTION PLAN:	M	T	W	T	F	S	S	%

EDUCATIONAL GOALS:					Accomplished		

Book:		Pgs.	Projected		Pgs.	Actual	

EDUCATIONAL GOALS ACTION PLAN:	M	T	W	T	F	S	S	%

PERSONAL GOALS:				Accomplished				

Book:		Pgs.	Projected		Pgs.	Actual		

PERSONAL GOALS ACTION PLAN:	M	T	W	T	F	S	S	%

BUSINESS/CAREER GOALS:				Accomplished				

Book:		Pgs.	Projected		Pgs.	Actual		

BUSINESS/CAREER GOALS ACTION PLAN:	M	T	W	T	F	S	S	%

RECREATIONAL GOALS:				Accomplished					

Book:		Pgs.	Projected		Pgs.	Actual			

RECREATIONAL GOALS ACTION PLAN:	M	T	W	T	F	S	S	%

CIVIC GOALS:				Accomplished					

Book:		Pgs.	Projected		Pgs.	Actual			

CIVIC GOALS ACTION PLAN:	M	T	W	T	F	S	S	%

CREATIVITY GOALS:				**Accomplished**				

Book:		Pgs.	Projected		Pgs.	Actual		

CREATIVITY GOALS ACTION PLAN:	**M**	**T**	**W**	**T**	**F**	**S**	**S**	**%**

This week's meeting place: _____ Date:_____

Attendees:

1. _____   4._____

2. _____   5._____

3. _____   6._____

Next week's meeting place: _____ Date:_____

Notes:

WEEKLY MASTERMIND PLAN

NAME: _____

FOR WEEK OF: _____

MEMORY SCRIPTURE or QUOTE FOR THE MONTH:

SPIRITUAL GOALS:	Accomplished

Book:	Pgs.	Projected		Pgs.	Actual

SPIRITUAL GOALS ACTION PLAN:	M	T	W	T	F	S	S	%

FAMILY GOALS:		Accomplished

Book:	Pgs.	Projected		Pgs.	Actual

FAMILY GOALS ACTION PLAN:	M	T	W	T	F	S	S	%

FINANCIAL GOALS:		Accomplished

Book:	Pgs.	Projected		Pgs.	Actual

FINANCIAL GOALS ACTION PLAN:	M	T	W	T	F	S	S	%

HEALTH GOALS:								Accomplished	

Book:		Pgs.	Projected		Pgs.	Actual			

HEALTH GOALS ACTION PLAN:	M	T	W	T	F	S	S	%

EDUCATIONAL GOALS:								Accomplished	

Book:		Pgs.	Projected		Pgs.	Actual			

EDUCATIONAL GOALS ACTION PLAN:	M	T	W	T	F	S	S	%

PERSONAL GOALS:		Accomplished

Book:	Pgs.	Projected	Pgs.	Actual

PERSONAL GOALS ACTION PLAN:	M	T	W	T	F	S	S	%

BUSINESS/CAREER GOALS:		Accomplished

Book:	Pgs.	Projected	Pgs.	Actual

BUSINESS/CAREER GOALS ACTION PLAN:	M	T	W	T	F	S	S	%

RECREATIONAL GOALS:		Accomplished

Book:	Pgs.	Projected		Pgs.	Actual

RECREATIONAL GOALS ACTION PLAN:	M	T	W	T	F	S	S	%

CIVIC GOALS:		Accomplished

Book:	Pgs.	Projected		Pgs.	Actual

CIVIC GOALS ACTION PLAN:	M	T	W	T	F	S	S	%

CREATIVITY GOALS:				Accomplished		
Book:	Pgs.	Projected		Pgs.	Actual	

CREATIVITY GOALS ACTION PLAN:	M	T	W	T	F	S	S	%

This week's meeting place: _____ Date:_____

Attendees:

1. _____   4._____

2. _____   5._____

3. _____   6._____

Next week's meeting place:_____ Date:_____

Notes:

WEEKLY MASTERMIND PLAN

NAME: _____

FOR WEEK OF: _____

MEMORY SCRIPTURE or QUOTE FOR THE MONTH:

SPIRITUAL GOALS:	Accomplished

Book:		Pgs.	Projected		Pgs.	Actual

SPIRITUAL GOALS ACTION PLAN:	M	T	W	T	F	S	S	%

FAMILY GOALS:				**Accomplished**

Book:	Pgs.	Projected		Pgs.	Actual

FAMILY GOALS ACTION PLAN:	M	T	W	T	F	S	S	%

FINANCIAL GOALS:				**Accomplished**

Book:	Pgs.	Projected		Pgs.	Actual

FINANCIAL GOALS ACTION PLAN:	M	T	W	T	F	S	S	%

HEALTH GOALS:		Accomplished

Book:	Pgs.	Projected		Pgs.	Actual

HEALTH GOALS ACTION PLAN:	M	T	W	T	F	S	S	%

EDUCATIONAL GOALS:		Accomplished

Book:	Pgs.	Projected		Pgs.	Actual

EDUCATIONAL GOALS ACTION PLAN:	M	T	W	T	F	S	S	%

PERSONAL GOALS:				**Accomplished**		

Book:		Pgs.	Projected		Pgs.	Actual

PERSONAL GOALS ACTION PLAN:	M	T	W	T	F	S	S	%

BUSINESS/CAREER GOALS:				**Accomplished**		

Book:		Pgs.	Projected		Pgs.	Actual

BUSINESS/CAREER GOALS ACTION PLAN:	M	T	W	T	F	S	S	%

RECREATIONAL GOALS:	Accomplished

Book:	Pgs.	Projected		Pgs.	Actual

RECREATIONAL GOALS ACTION PLAN:	M	T	W	T	F	S	S	%

CIVIC GOALS:	Accomplished

Book:	Pgs.	Projected		Pgs.	Actual

CIVIC GOALS ACTION PLAN:	M	T	W	T	F	S	S	%

CREATIVITY GOALS:		Accomplished

Book:	Pgs.	Projected		Pgs.	Actual

CREATIVITY GOALS ACTION PLAN:	**M**	**T**	**W**	**T**	**F**	**S**	**S**	**%**

This week's meeting place: _____ Date:_____

Attendees:

    1. _____   4._____

    2. _____   5._____

    3. _____   6._____

Next week's meeting place:_____ Date:_____

Notes:

WEEKLY MASTERMIND PLAN

NAME: _____

FOR WEEK OF: _____

MEMORY SCRIPTURE or QUOTE FOR THE MONTH:

SPIRITUAL GOALS:	Accomplished

Book:	Pgs.	Projected		Pgs.	Actual

SPIRITUAL GOALS ACTION PLAN:	M	T	W	T	F	S	S	%

FAMILY GOALS:		**Accomplished**

Book:	Pgs.	Projected		Pgs.	Actual

FAMILY GOALS ACTION PLAN:	**M**	**T**	**W**	**T**	**F**	**S**	**S**	**%**

FINANCIAL GOALS:		**Accomplished**

Book:	Pgs.	Projected		Pgs.	Actual

FINANCIAL GOALS ACTION PLAN:	**M**	**T**	**W**	**T**	**F**	**S**	**S**	**%**

HEALTH GOALS:						**Accomplished**			

Book:		Pgs.	Projected		Pgs.	Actual			

HEALTH GOALS ACTION PLAN:	M	T	W	T	F	S	S	%

EDUCATIONAL GOALS:						**Accomplished**			

Book:		Pgs.	Projected		Pgs.	Actual			

EDUCATIONAL GOALS ACTION PLAN:	M	T	W	T	F	S	S	%

PERSONAL GOALS:				Accomplished	

Book:	Pgs.	Projected		Pgs.	Actual

PERSONAL GOALS ACTION PLAN:	M	T	W	T	F	S	S	%

BUSINESS/CAREER GOALS:				Accomplished	

Book:	Pgs.	Projected		Pgs.	Actual

BUSINESS/CAREER GOALS ACTION PLAN:	M	T	W	T	F	S	S	%

RECREATIONAL GOALS:								Accomplished	

Book:		Pgs.	Projected		Pgs.	Actual			

RECREATIONAL GOALS ACTION PLAN:	M	T	W	T	F	S	S	%

CIVIC GOALS:								Accomplished	

Book:		Pgs.	Projected		Pgs.	Actual			

CIVIC GOALS ACTION PLAN:	M	T	W	T	F	S	S	%

CREATIVITY GOALS:									**Accomplished**	

Book:		Pgs.	Projected		Pgs.	Actual

CREATIVITY GOALS ACTION PLAN:	M	T	W	T	F	S	S	%

This week's meeting place: _____ Date:_____

Attendees:

1. _____   4._____

2. _____   5._____

3. _____   6._____

Next week's meeting place: _____ Date:_____

Notes:

Appendix A
New Groups Welcome Kit

Dear Group Members:

Welcome to the heart and soul of masterminding. You have formed a group. Having a group of like-minded people holding you accountable for accomplishing your dreams, goals, and aspirations has proven to be the success of countless notable moguls.

Ann Mcneill has had over 35 years of masterminding experience and has found what works well and best. Using the proven guidelines provided will help your group excel.

Please know that as time and circumstances change, your group will change too. That's okay - expect it, embrace it, and hold true to your group's mission statement. Be sure to make your group's operational and accountability guidelines clear and honor them at all times. Also stay true to the accountability guidelines and member code of ethics and policies. Embrace the experience. You'll be glad you did!

Your group leader has agreed to give you the support needed to help you acquire all that you have identified as important; be sure to return the favor by rendering support to them in return.

Welcome to the McNeill Factor. We wish you and your group great success.

Sincerely,

Ann McNeill

Ann McNeill
The Master Builder

How to Form a MasterMind Group

CHECKLIST: HOW TO FORM GROUP

FIRST MEETING – SUGGESTED AGENDA

WHY MASTERMIND?

HISTORY AND FOUNDER

MEMBER CODE OF ETHICS

MEMBER POLICIES (ACCOUNTABILITY)

GROUPS REGISTRATION FORM

INDIVIDUAL MEMBERSHIP APPLICATION

NOTES:

Checklist How to Form a Group

✔ Review proceeding pages titled *Why MasterMind, History and Founder, and Member Code of Ethics and Accountability*.

✔ Plan the first meeting (approximately 1 ½ to 2 hours).
   o Pick a location for the meeting (or choose date/time if virtual group formation).
   o Invite and confirm at least three people for the meeting.
   o Confirm attendance of a Group Advisor.
   o Give a copy of each of these to each guest: *Why MasterMind?, History and Founder,* and *Member Code of Ethics and Member Policies (Accountability)*.

✔ Hold the first meeting (facilitated by a Group Advisor). An Advisor can be assigned by contacting the membership committee.

✔ At the first meeting be prepared to –
   o Decide on the next group meeting date.
   o Decide on a group leader. (Just because you initiate the first meeting does not mean you have to be the group leader. One of the other people may take on this role.)
   o Go over the enclosed *MasterMind Group Registration Form* and set a date to submit the completed form, along with the one-time group registration fee.
   o Agree on a weekly call schedule with Group Advisor for the first eight weeks after group formation.
   o Set dates to follow the suggested *Think and Grow Rich* reading schedule or agree and set dates to follow a different schedule.
   o Decide on a group name (which must be on the Group Registration form).

✔ Complete the weekly calls with the Groups Advisor that are set up during the first meeting.

✔ Submit the completed Group Registration form with fee to your Group Advisor within 30 days of the first group meeting.

✔ Submit a completed ***Membership Form***, along with membership fee, for each group member to your Group Advisor, within 30 days of the first group meeting.

✔ Each member confirms to the group leader that after submitting their membership application and required fee they received a *New Member MasterMind Workbook* along with a copy of *Think and Grow Rich.*

Suggested Agenda - First Meeting

FIRST MEETING - SUGGESTED AGENDA

Please keep in mind:

The assigned TMF Advisor facilitates this meeting and may have a standard agenda for first meetings that may be used in place of or with adjustments to this suggested agenda.

I. Call to order and Prayer/Meditation

II. Introductions by everyone

III. Advisor goes over information on these pages, answering any questions
   a. TMF History and Founder
   b. Why MasterMind?
   c. TMF Member Code of Ethics and TMF Member Policies (Accountability)

IV. Advisor goes over the Groups Registration Form; and the group agrees on a date to submit the form with the required fee

V. The Advisor will discuss the roles members may take within the group
   a. Group Leader, Chaplain, Secretary, Assistant to any of these if group prefers
   b. Group will decide on Group Leader

VI. Agree on weekly "coaching" call dates with Advisor for next eight weeks (e.g. Thursdays, 7p-8p)

VII. Agree on date for everyone to submit TMF membership application and dues

VIII. Decide on a group name

IX. Set the date for the next group face-to-face meeting

X. Any wrap up discussion

XI. Closing Prayer/Meditation and Adjournment

NOTES:

Why MasterMind?

The objective of the MasterMind approach is to show accountability. Weekly meetings and group discussions regarding specific goals facilitate each member's accountability for accomplishing set goals. You must have goals AND action plans to achieve these goals if you are going to succeed in any endeavor. Successful people make and work their plans.

Success consists of three ingredients:

1. **Direction**
   - Set your sights on things that are worthwhile in life.
   - Establish a plan.
   - Continually work toward fulfillment and accomplishment of set goals and plans.

2. **Balance**
   - Keep the proper perspective about every area of your life.
   - Stay in harmony with God's Holy Spirit and guidance, which produces perfect balance .Balance in all things produces joy.

3. **Belief**
   - The stronger your belief is in your success the more you work to complete your goals No one will become successful if they do not possess belief in that success
   - Each completed step brings a degree of success.
   - Great people have strong beliefs!

By consistently using the MasterMind approach in every area of your life, you can achieve your goals!

NOTES:

History and Founder

The premise on which the McNeill Factor (TMF) is based originated within the pages of Napoleon Hill's book, Think and Grow Rich, in which he explained the MasterMind principle. MasterMind is an organization of like-minded people who use this principle to set and meet goals.

On the eve of a new year, a new era in life was ushered in for Ann McNeill. On December 31, 1980 instead of enjoying the New Year's Eve festivities out and about, Ann McNeill decided to stay home and read a book. That book was Napoleon Hill's *Think and Grow Rich* and it changed her life. The book soon became her "bible" of sorts and like any religious zealot she took her "bible" with her everywhere she went. She "preached" its principles to anyone that would listen. She gave the book to a small circle of friends at her local church in West Palm Beach, FL and from there began to give the book as a gift for birthdays.

In *Think and Grow Rich* Ann McNeill was introduced to the MasterMind concept of goal setting. Once she started to apply the principles in the book to her own life, a shift began to take place. She began to move from mediocrity to excellence. She also realized that it would be selfish of her to keep the MasterMind concept to herself, and that a big part of MasterMind is accountability. She needed to share MasterMind with others; she needed a group of like-minded people to whom she would be accountable. She began to meet in discussion sessions with those to whom she had given the book. From this the original *MasterMind Women's Group* was formed.

As Ann McNeill's life transitioned so did the group. Her move to Miami, FL in the early 1990s meant the formation of a MasterMind group in Miami. The original Miami MasterMind women included Alice Fincher, Bert Johnson, Isabella Rivers, Shuandra Scott, Nifretta Thomas and, of course, Ann McNeill. The group quickly expanded to include five more ladies (Gail Seay, Juanita Dawsey, Lawanda Scott, Tanya Jackson, and Mia Merritt), all of whom cemented and held together over the next decade. For ten years, this group met every Saturday morning at seven to discuss their goals, while experiencing tremendous growth in membership. McNeill herself left her corporate job to start a construction company, MCO Construction & Services; which she parlayed into a small dynasty as she is now also president of MCO Consulting, Inc., Constructively Speaking, Inc., a Colbert/Ball Tax Franchise and Speak 2 Share, Inc.

The MasterMind Women's Group saw members come and go, but the nucleus and the precepts on which it was founded remained. In 2005, the group restructured and the *MasterMind Empowerment Association* was born; and with this more formal organization, membership grew to nearly one hundred members, including men and children for the first time. At the same time, the organization's annual meeting was restructured into an annual conference. Then, in 2007 the organization began another makeover, changing its name to the *International MasterMind Association, Inc.* (IMA) to encompass membership that has spread from the United States to the Caribbean. To date, the original group has produced several authors, including Dr. Mia Y. Merritt, as well as a host of successful entrepreneurs.

TMF Member Code of Ethics

TMF Member CODE OF ETHICS

- I will always contribute to the harmonious supportive atmosphere of my group/chapter.

- I will encourage and be non-judgmental of my fellow members.

- I am committed to my own dreams and goals as well as my fellow members' success.

- I will work to compassionately hold my group members accountable to the goals that they have set for themselves

- I will always behave ethically toward my group members and the other members of TMF.

- I will maintain absolute confidentiality with respect to the disclosures made by my fellow members.

- I will always seek to expand my knowledge base; and

- I will consistently MasterMind, with the understanding that each group/chapter relies on my conscientious attendance and participation.

NOTES:

Member Policies (Accountability)

MEMBER POLICIES

- Prior to the submission of an application, potential members may attend one group meeting.

- Membership within a group occurs once all admission requirements have been met, and with the unanimous vote by group members accepting membership; with the provision that the Group Leader may overturn a membership vote to accept a member at their discretion.

- Membership dues are to be paid annually on or before January 31st of each year. New members must pay dues on the date of admission. Member dues is pro-rated when a member comes in mid-year.

- Only active, non-provisional members can be elected to serve on committees, receive member discounts, appear in the membership directory, have mentor assignments, and participate in the MasterMind Advisor certificate program.

- Members are expected to arrive at meetings or events in a timely manner and to remain for the duration.

- Attendance is critical to group meetings. Upon the third absence from group meetings within any three-month period of a calendar year (January to December), a member shall be placed on probation and, at the direction of the Group Leader, may have his or her membership revoked due to lack of participation.

- A medical absence or leave of absence is allowed, if prior notice is provided to, and approval is obtained from the Group Leader.

- A member may belong to more than one MasterMind group.

- A member may be reinstated to a group upon the submission of a written request for reinstatement followed by a unanimous vote by group members to allow reinstatement; with the provision that the Group Leader may overturn a vote and reinstate a member at their discretion.

- A member transferring from one group to another must complete a Transfer Form and acceptance into the requested group is contingent upon a unanimous vote by group members accepting the member; with the provision that the Group Leader may overturn a vote relating to the transfer and accept a transferring member at their discretion. Please ask membership about this form.

- Any member with a grievance/conflict should contact the Group Leader for resolution.

- All member lists/contact resources are for the purpose of MasterMinding and may not be used for solicitation in any format (i.e. e-mail, direct mail or other means), nor otherwise disclosed to any non-member without member prior approval.

Group Registration Form

NOTES:

Appendix B
How to Form a
MasterMind Group
and
How to Run an Effective Meeting

Running Effective MasterMind Meetings

After the initial group meeting, the Group Leader is responsible for planning and facilitating effective meetings for the group. The second group meeting after the initial meeting with the certified Group Advisor will need to address items as outlined in the Agenda below. To prepare for this meeting, each group member should have completed the annual survey, self contract, submitted their Membership Application with required fee, and completed the first reading assignment for *Think and Grow Rich*. Plan for a meeting length of 1½ to 2 hours.

SAMPLE AGENDA - SECOND GROUP MEETING
MasterMind Group Meeting for "Group Name"

Date:_____ Time:_____ Location:_____

I.   Call to Order and Opening Prayer/Meditation

II.   Recite Member Code of Ethics in unison

III.   Discuss and Submit completed/signed documents to Group Leader with copies (originals to Group Advisor)
    a.   Self Contract
    b.   Annual Survey
    c.   Membership Application and fee of any group member still outstanding)

IV.   With Group Advisor
    a.   Review How to Use the MasterMind Workbook
    b.   Complete the *Think and Grow Rich* Questionnaire
    c.   Discuss Affirmation and Personal Affirmation
    d.   Discuss How to Create Goals

V.   Discuss/Finalize
    a.   Meeting dates, locations, time options, including next meeting
    b.   Attendance Policy Agreement to be used by group
        (see Member Policies page 141

c.   Accountability Guidelines and Acknowledgement to be used by group
       (see page 141)

VI.   Discuss completed reading assignment for *Think and Grow Rich* (this was assigned by
        Advisor during one of your calls, just to get the group started)

VII.   Agree on reading schedule for the rest of the Think & Grow Rich book or follow the
        suggested schedule included in these pages

VIII.   Confirm Homework due next meeting
        a.   As assigned by Group Advisor
        b.   *Think and Grow Rich* reading assignment from agreed upon schedule

IX.   Closing Prayer/Meditation and Adjournment

Running Effective MasterMind Meetings

Ideally, the third group meeting occurs once all eight of the weekly calls with the advisor have been completed. After this third meeting, the group meeting agenda should be standard. A sample agenda for this third group meeting as well as a sample agenda for a standard MasterMind group meeting after 90-days follow on these pages. Third meeting should take about 1½ to 2 hours. After this meetings should take about 1 to 1½ hours, depending on the agenda and how the meeting is conducted

SAMPLE AGENDA - THIRD GROUP MEETING
MasterMind Group Meeting for "Group Name"

Date:_____ Time:_____ Location:_____

I.   Call to Order and Opening Prayer/Meditation

II.   Recite Code of Ethics in Unison

III.   Submit to Group Leader with copies for Group Advisor
        a.   Signed Group Attendance Agreement
        b.   Signed Group Accountability Guidelines and Acknowledgement

IV.   Discuss completed *Think and Grow Rich* reading assignment

V.   Discuss each members finalized goals and personal affirmation

VI.   Discuss Income Circles

VII.   Discuss Booklist and decide which books the group will read for the rest of year

VIII.   Confirm next meeting date/time/location from agreed upon schedule

IX.   Confirm next scheduled reading assignment

X.   Adjourn with closing prayer/meditation

NOTES:

Running Effective MasterMind Meetings

SAMPLE STANDARD AGENDA - MASTERMIND GROUP MEETING
"Group Name"

Date:_____ Time:_____ Location:_____

I.   Call to Order and Opening prayer/meditation

II.   Recite Code of Ethics in unison

III.   Make any reports as needed (e.g. if member assigned project, task; report progress here)

IV.   Read personal affirmations

V.   Share progress on action plans for goals since last meeting (discuss challenges, solutions as needed)

VI.   Finalize any discussions from previous meeting as appropriate

VII.   Discuss any business
        a.   Group Leader Report (due first Mondays)
        b.   Upcoming events (e.g. Mid-Year, Annual Conference, etc.)
        c.   Other

VIII.   Discuss completed reading assignment

IX.   Confirm next scheduled reading assignment and next meeting date/time/location

X.   Adjourn with closing prayer/meditation

GROUP LEADER: TIPS FOR RUNNING EFFECTIVE MEETINGS

✔ Make sure you have everything you will need for the upcoming meeting

✔ Confirm meeting logistics with all attendees

- ✔ Circulate an agenda to all attendees at least 24 hours before meeting date/time
  - o Agenda should indicate meeting time limit
  - o Suggestion: indicate time limit for each agenda item such as reports, discussions
  - o Make sure agenda items are listed in order of priority (most important items before less important items (and when needed allot more time to these more important items)

- ✔ Start and end the meeting at the agreed upon times

- ✔ Keep the meeting moving by
  - o following the agenda
  - o redirecting off-topic discussions back to agenda topics
  - o staying within established time limits for each agenda item

Monthly Group Reporting Form

GROUP REPORT FORM

Name of MasterMind Group	Date Established

Name of Person Providing Report:

Date Completed:

General Information

Type of Group:	Adult	Youth

Name of Group Leader:

Number of Members	
Frequency of Meeting	
Type of Meeting	

Greatest Accomplishments Last Month

One rose (something good):

One thorn (roadblock):

One major lesson learned on behalf of the group:

NOTES:

TMF Annual Programming

TMF MID-YEAR MEETING - Summer each year

Members provide a mid-year report of their progress, including an updated TMF survey, accomplishments and challenges in completing action steps toward goals. Members participate in activities and development sessions to facilitate life goals and becoming the best YOU. Registration and site information is typically provided at the annual conference and is available on line at www.internationalmasterminders.com.

TMF ANNUAL CONFERENCE - January each year

Members typically pre-register for this conference and also renew their TMF membership before the conference date. Members benefit from conference speakers, workshops and small group interactions that focused on achieving life goals. Members provide an annual report of their goals for previous year; submit completed annual survey of that year, along with goals and action plans for the new year.

Other annual programming can include Golf and Scholarship events, special member workshops (e.g. goal setting; writing a book; becoming professional speaker). Details will be provided in TMF emails, on the Google group site, and/or at the website.

NOTES:

_____
_____
_____
_____
_____
_____
_____
_____
_____
_____
_____
_____
_____
_____
_____
_____
_____
_____
_____
_____
_____
_____
_____
_____
_____
_____
_____
_____
_____
_____
_____
_____

Suggested Think and Grow Rich Reading Schedule

The following reading schedule is a guide. Your group may decide to read more chapters each week to complete the book in less time or you may choose to read 1 chapter per month. The goal is to consistently progress through the foundational text for successful masterminding, while ensuring each group member understands how to integrate the principles and precepts of masterminding into their life.

Week	Assigned Reading for *Think and Grow Rich* by Napoleon Hill
1	Introduction and Chapter 1
2	Chapter 2
3	Chapter 3
4	Chapter 4
5	Chapter 5
6	Chapter 6
7	Chapters 7 and 8
8	Chapter 9
9	Chapter 10
10	Chapter 11
11	Chapter 12
12	Epilogue

HOW TO USE YOUR WORKBOOK

Let's begin with YOU. You need to USE your workbook. Begin by taking ownership – complete the information page in the front of your TMF workbook. Now, review the table of contents and visit each section shown there to become familiar with your New Member TMF workbook. It is so tempting to jump right in to the part of the workbook we like best, but let's follow the process so you will receive the most benefit.

Masterminding is all about accountability. So in cooperation with the members of your group, and the experience offered by veteran masterminders, use your workbook consistently, to help you set goals, develop and use a plan of action; make adjustments, and identify areas in which you require additional support and/or resources to help you get around road blocks.

If you do not yet have a group affiliation, then consider your option to begin your own group (see the Appendix B for step by step instructions) or just ask someone in the membership committee about joining an existing group, open to new members.

MasterMind Book List

As mentioned before knowledge is power, and reading is fundamental to obtaining that knowledge. MasterMind encourages all its members to read. There are two books that are mandatory reading for membership with MasterMind. Those books are, of course, *Think and Grow Rich* and *Success: The Glenn Bland Method.* Other books that MasterMind suggests that you read are on the following pages:

BOOK	AUTHOR	CATEGORY	% READ

NOTES:

_____

_____

_____

_____

_____

_____

_____

_____

_____

_____

_____

_____

_____

_____

_____

_____

_____

_____

_____

_____

_____

_____

_____

_____

_____

_____

_____

_____

_____

MasterMind Suggested Reading List

1. The Bible
2. *As a Man Thinketh* by Allen James
3. *The Magic of Thinking Big* by David J. Schwartz
4. *The Magic of Believing* by Claude Bristol
5. *The Greatest Salesman in the World* by Og Mandino
6. *How To Win Friends and Influence People* by Dale Carnegie
7. *Acres of Diamonds* by Russell H. Conwell
8. *Psycho-Cybernetics* by Maxwell Maltz
9. *Move Ahead with Possibility Thinking* by Robert Schuller
10. *Think and Grow Rich* by Napoleon Hill
11. *The Richest Man in Babylon* by George Clason
12. *I am - I can* by Daniel Steered
13. *Who is this Man Jesus? Edited* by Kenneth N. Taylor
14. *The Magic Power of Self Image Psychology* by Maxwell Maltz
15. *Self-love The Dynamic Force of Success* by Robert H. Schuller
16. *Wake up and Live* by Dorothea Brande
17. *God's Psychiatry* by Charles L. Allen
18. *Grow Rich with Peace of Mind* by Napoleon Hill
19. *God, Money and You* by George Otis
20. *Improving Your Self-image* by Norman Wright
21. *Life is Tremendous* by Charlie "Tremendous" Jones
22. *The Art of Loving* by Erich Fromm
23. *Key to Yourself* by Venice Bloodworth
24. *Believe!* By Richard M. Devos
25. *The Purpose Driven Life* by Rick Warren
26. *The Friendship Factor* by Alan L. McGinnis
27. *Daily Guide to a Better Marriage* by Donald Moore
28. *Investment Guide* by Kiasoshi
29. *Don't Worry Make Money* by Richard Carlson

30. *Finish Rich Workbook* by David Bach

31. *Creating Affluence* by Deepak Chopra

32. *Investment Guide* by Andrew P. Tobias

33. *Power of Focus* by Jack Canifield, Les Hewitt, Mark Victor Hansen

34. *How to Retire* by Robert T. Kiyosaki & Sharon L. Leenter

35. *Finish Rich Workbook* by David Bach

36. *Great Quotes* by Zig Ziglar

37. *Your Body's Many Cries for Water* by Dr. F. Batmageli

38. *Fit For Life* by Pamela Peeke

39. *Herbs for Over 50* - Unknown Author

40. *It Only Takes a Minute* by Willie Jolley

41. *Random Acts of Kindness* by Daphne Rose Kingma and Dawna Markova

42. *Ten Secrets for the Man in the Mirror* by Patrick Morley

43. *Running a Successful Construction Company* by David Grerstel

44. *Natural Healing* by Mark Bricklin

45. *My Tongue Needs Healing* by Derek Prince

46. *Miseducation of the Negro* by Carter Godwin Woodson

47. *Good to Great* by James C. Collins

48. *Life of Tiger Woods* by Earl Woods and Pete McDaniel

49. *Personal Summers and Power Surges* by Bettye Lewis

50. *Attitude of Gratitude* by M. J. Ryan

51. *Is There a Cause* by Joseph Tosini

52. *Knowing Your Strengths* - Author Unknown

53. *Start Late Finish Rich at Any Age* by David Bach

54. *Confessions of Happy Christian* by Zig Ziglar

55. *What Momma taught Me* by Tony Brown

56. *The Spirit of Leadership* by Miles Munroe

57. *Die Broke* by Mark Levine, Stephen M. Pollan

58. *If Life is a Game These are the Rules* by Cherie Carter-Scott

For more information please contact:

Constructively Speaking
1450 North Mangonia Drive
West Palm Beach, Florida, 33401
Phone: 786-546-0184
Fax: 305-693-4544
Email: ann@annmcneill.com

About the Founder
Ann McNeill

Ann McNeill is a proud graduate of Florida Memorial University and Founder of the Ann McNeill MasterMind Method. For more than 30 years, members within TMF have been partnering to support one another for success. TMF is a unique group of likeminded individuals who collectively, embrace the distinguishing qualities necessary for success -- ownership and accountability. In addition, Mrs. McNeill is also the Founder of MCO Construction & Services, Inc., a full service construction company dedicated to delivering projects on-time, within budget, and in compliance with the special needs of large public and private projects. MCO has performed construction with a combined value in excess of $110 million. In an industry with few black- or female-run companies, MCO Construction is a standout example of possibilities. "MCO is a small company with a large presence!"

Ann McNeill is an innovative community activist, a pioneer in the field of youth and adult investment clubs for African Americans, a noted speaker, and a proud mother and wife. Her career has been built one challenge and one opportunity at a time.

DREAM LIST	COMMENTS

www.ingramcontent.com/pod-product-compliance
Lightning Source LLC
Chambersburg PA
CBHW081434190326

41458CB00020B/6202